CONNECT

Learn to Connect with...

- **Yourself**

- **Others**

- **The World**

Jacob B. Goettsche

Published by
Silver Eagle Publishing,

Washington, Utah

Copyright © 2023 by Jacob B. Goettsche

All rights reserved. No part of this book may be reproduced or transmitted in any form or by any means, electronic, or mechanical, including photocopying, recording, or by any information storage and retrieval system, or any manner without written permission of the copyright owner except for the use of quotations in a book review. For more information, email: cubephilosophy888@gmail.com.

First paperback edition June 2023

ISBN 978-1-60655-059-5 (paperback)
ISBN 978-1-60655-060-1 (eBook)
https://www.theconnectioncube.com

FOREWARD

In life, most, if not all of us, seek some type of truth. In this respect, Jacob is no different. However, what is different is how he seeks to understand truth. In that way, he also seeks to understand how we all relate to one another. You may or may not agree with the approach he takes, but, regardless, you will find it insightful and worthy of your time and consideration.

In many ways, "Connect" is a deeply spiritual and philosophical book, but not a religious one necessarily. Hence, the name "cube philosophy." Jacob attempts to dissect human thought patterns to understand himself, others, and the world around him. He is led to a cube structure and with this metaphor concludes that much of what we understand, do, experience, etc. is often a matter of perspective.

Jacob, for example, might say that some see a glass partially filled with liquid as half full, some may see it as half empty, and some may see it both ways. Thus, Jacob raises a number of paradoxes that confront human understanding and explains to us how they exist.

I confess that I am probably more inclined to see the glass as half empty. Jacob teaches us to try to see it both ways, although he strikes me as someone who usually sees the glass as half full. What we should learn from his introspection, however, is to nearly always, if not always, seek the opposite or opposing view of how we are naturally inclined to interpret others and the world around us to experience and appreciate our own existence more fully.

This is without a doubt excellent advice. The discourse of how Jacob gets there is intriguing, and especially of some importance at a time when following a worldwide pandemic, we all feel a bit more disconnected than before the pandemic.

~**Howard Skaist**

ACKNOWLEDGMENTS

FIRST I would like to thank John Ward for encouraging me to write about my philosophy. As he told me later, "If I had to listen to you talk to me about your cube again, without doing something with it, I was going to get angry with you." John inspired me to reveal my mind to the world and share what I have learned throughout my life.

SECOND I want to thank Chris, EJ, Dean, Christie, Kevin, Will, Dave, and my daughter Olivia for reading my rough draft, and helping me evolve my book into what it is today.

THIRD I want to thank editor William Bosley for asking great questions and offering his expert advice.

FOURTH I want to thank my dear friend Joshua Awesome for listening and for being there for me. I couldn't have done it without you!

FIFTH I owe my mom a debt of gratitude that goes beyond words. The obvious reason is because she brought me into this world. Though, occasionally she would jokingly say, "Hey, I brought you into this world, and I can take you out!" Thank you for raising me with kindness, patience, and love. You talked with me about deep truths and riddles. You helped me learn how to think and ask good questions. One saying she would repeat often, "People see life in a mirror, Jake." You were an amazing single mom, and I want to let you know how grateful I am for your exceptional example. Also, thanks for helping put the final edits on the book and helping me format my manuscript.

SIXTH Thank you to all of those I shared my idea with and encouraged me to keep on going. One man that comes to mind is Shawn, who I met at the Bloc Yard in Spokane, WA . Thank you for volunteering to donate to my project. The fact that you offered without me asking, helped me to believe even more that I was on the right track.

CONTENTS

CHAPTER 1
Truth is a Paradox 1

CHAPTER 2
Unscrambling Truth 5

CHAPTER 3
Truth in Numbers and Colors 17

CHAPTER 4
Shared Truth 23

CHAPTER 5
Knowledge is Mainly Objective 41

CHAPTER 6
Influence is Mainly Subjective 53

CHAPTER 7
The Quest for the Optimal Shared Truth 67

CHAPTER 8
Please Take the Paradox Pill 89
Rules for Cube Philosophy 90

CHAPTER 1
Truth is a Paradox

Truth seems to be as elusive as a unicorn, Bigfoot, or the Loch Ness monster. Some people claim to have seen them, others doubt their existence, and others can't see, or refuse to see, how they even have a bearing on their lives, even if they were proven to be real. The whole endeavor appears highly speculative, and yet we see their likeness in the objective world. Are these creatures real because we have evidence of horses, dinosaur bones, or large apes? Which leaves many in a state of wonder, mystery, and riddle. Is it possible for them to be real, and not real, at the same time?

Why do we have the word paradox, and what does it mean? According to Oxford languages, "A paradox is a seemingly absurd or self-contradictory statement or proposition that when investigated or explained may prove to be well founded or true."

In the next six chapters, I hope to prove that the Truth is both objective and subjective in the truest sense possible. Cube philosophy sets out to unscramble this mystery by providing evidence that the best way to perceive Truth, is that we must think of it as having more than one face. Truth, in fact, has six faces and yet is one. Like how the body has many members, and yet is one body. Unless we accept that Truth is a paradox to begin with, it will remain as elusive as a unicorn.

> **Truth, in fact, has six faces and yet is one.**

One of the first taught paradoxes is the liar paradox. The liar who says that they are lying is, in fact, telling the truth about being a liar. The way I like to think of it is the fact that someone told a lie now makes it part of Truth. Why? Because the lie actually exists in truth and yet is still a lie. Tell that lie long and loud enough in reality, and it becomes true. The old expression of someone who believes their own lie.

My favorite paradoxical quote is about relationships. "With people, fast is slow, and slow is fast." A reminder that trust and understanding are built over time.

Another paradox is you and I looking at a cube opposite each other with six colors on it, and I ask, "Which side is the color orange on?" The color is both on the left and right, without contradicting ourselves, because perspective is the main factor that makes it so. Like asking the person in the mirror to raise their right hand. Scream all day long that they are only raising their left hand, but it won't do you any good. To understand how complex and simple Truth is, you must accept that Truth, itself, is a paradox.

CHAPTER 2
Unscrambling Truth

Cube philosophy was created by observing many elements of my life and others' lives. One of these elements included reading hundreds of ancient to modern texts of a philosophical and religious nature. One of the books I read was *The 7 Habits of Highly Effective People* by Stephen R. Covey. I believe his work touches on a lot of the actual Truth we all share. You may notice some of his Influence on this philosophy.

NOTE: **As you read along, you will see I capitalize specific words. This is to emphasize the words' importance or to convey an idea. For example, when speaking of the one Truth we all share, I use a capital "T." When speaking of someone's personal truth, or a piece of truth, I use the lower case "t."**

Let me assure you reader, I am not saying I know what the Truth is. What I am calling "Cube Philosophy" is only offering a way to see the complex Truth, reduced to one simple shape, in the hope that we will genuinely connect for the right reasons.

Since I don't want to catch you off-guard, I need to let you know that I am going to reveal moments of my own life in this book. That way you know I am not above or below anyone, I'm just standing next to you trying to live out my life in harmony with yours. To do that effectively means I have to factor in many variables, but exactly how many variables are there?

This is my story of how I discovered the six minor truths, to help me simplify and try to understand the one major Truth.

When I was a younger man, I arrogantly thought I had the Truth. I believed my religion was right, because of the spiritual experiences I'd had and the knowledge I'd obtained. I studied what I thought was broad enough to gain insight, but, in reality, I had only played in lakes and rivers without having as yet experienced the ocean. Neither was I factoring in everyone else's lived experiences, which compounds the problem even more.

I was married back then. My wife and I started to suspect that our two-year-old son was not normal. After a few examinations, we discovered that he is, in fact, mentally handicapped. He was often sick and later was diagnosed with epilepsy. As new parents, we didn't quite know how to help him. We tried many different things, but nothing really seemed to work.

Being raised without my father, I was really looking forward to being there for my son the way my father wasn't there for me. Upon learning my son was never going to be normal, my expectations were taken from me. I wasn't going to be able to teach him and connect the way I wanted to. He would never have a family or wife of his own. My line would end with him. My wife didn't understand what I was feeling, so I came across as very selfish. I was also trying to understand why God would do such a thing.

Striving to get a handle on my emotions, I started searching and studying, while trying to guide and provide for my family. I started to question the religion I was in, and I did eventually doubt that religion as well as my spiritual experiences.

After studying more, and having a different "spiritual experience," I ended up joining a different religion. My wife remained with the other one, which strained our marriage even further. I wanted to discuss what I was seeing and learning, but as I looked back, that wasn't really the case. I wanted to tell her how it would be and didn't consider how she might be feeling at that time.

She ran from the conversations, and eventually one night I blew up and came face to face with the monster I can be. In the moment that I screamed and felt the anger in my eyes, I frightened not only my wife and kids, but myself. I didn't know I could behave that way. I did immediately apologize. Still, the thought remained. If I didn't know I could get that angry, what else didn't I know? What else had my arrogance blinded me too?

As I spent the next couple of years trying to understand and fix myself, I realized how difficult it was. Who had the answers and where were they to be found? Most conversations I had ended with, "Well that's your Truth, and this is my Truth." The problem was that I intuitively knew that no one is entitled to their own Truth. Which meant there must be a common Truth we all share.

There must be a common Truth we all share.

For instance, say we walk up to a five-story building and jump off. Is it True you or I can fly, simply because we believe it to be so? Can either one of us hold our breaths indefinitely because we believe we no longer need air to live this human existence? No. How long can we go without food or water? We all have our limits.

That said, why did my ex-wife's grandmother choose one religion, and my mom decided to be a different religion? Because they both had personal experiences that made them believe in those religions. Who am I to say if those experiences are true or not? I love to skate, and enjoy various kinds of music, while other people prefer to hike, bike, or go to the gym. Why does the sight of blood cause some to feel nauseous, and others just want to help stop the bleeding? One person is yelled at and feels weaker, another person is yelled at and becomes stronger.

That's when I realized there is a subjective reality we are all experiencing, as well as an objective one.

Having arrived at this point in my journey, the adventure to discover *real* Truth began.

I could then see that I did have "my truth" and everyone else had "their truth." So, instead of trying to think of billions of truths, I reduced it down to "My Reality" and "Another's Reality." In fact, I have what is real to me, and you have what is real to you, hence real-ality.

> **I started to realize there is a subjective reality we are all experiencing, as well as an objective one.**

From there, I considered what other facets of Truth there are, and how do I rightly put them in their place?

I kept working and thinking about these questions in my mind, until one day I realized that "Knowledge" is something I don't own, and neither do you. As far as I can see, there are only two kinds of Knowledge. Knowledge that we use, and Knowledge of what is. Therefore, we have the sayings such as, "It is what it is" and "Do you know how to do that?"

Case in point: The planet we call earth, with the environment it provides, is Knowledge that exists outside of you and I. When I go to work, I use the Knowledge of driving, framing, roofing, geometry, laws, physics, social norms and more to navigate through each day, and you use Knowledge too.

Now, I felt confident there was My Reality which is one face, Another's Reality that makes two faces, and Knowledge, three faces of Truth. I pondered these in my mind, trying to see if there were more faces to Truth.

> **Now, I felt confident there was My Reality which is one face, Another's Reality that makes two faces, and Knowledge, three faces of Truth.**

As my life went on, I noticed we all seem to be Influenced by things which can be objectively observed as well as subjectively experienced. I can have Knowledge of how hot the sun is, that it exists, but then how does the sun cause me to sweat, get a sunburn, or potentially heatstroke if I stay in it long enough? How about when we watch someone perform at the pinnacle of perfection? Those actions have the potential to inspire some to try, and others aren't even impressed. Music is extremely Influential. Those beats and lyrics have the power to affect us in many ways. Movies and stories have Influence too. Do you recall the movie *It's a Wonderful Life?* The main message in that film is that just by existing we Influence the world around us, and the world Influences us too. I concluded that "Influence" must be another facet of Truth.

I spent several weeks mixing these four truths in my mind, to see if that could account for all the Truth that is in the world. It seemed to get close, but something felt like it was missing, some objective or subjective factor wasn't there yet. So, I went about living my life working through my daily problems, as we all do.

> **I concluded that "Influence" must be another facet of Truth.**

Then one day in conversation, I noticed we humans talk a lot about good and evil, right and wrong. We have been debating these questions of right and wrong for thousands of years. Some say that it is all in the mind, a subjective reality, but then you can pose the question, "Are you saying someone can come over to your house tonight, do unspeakable things to your family, then frame you for it, and that's fine, because you can't tell me they did anything wrong? Right?" Well, you would say back, "You mean what is objectively right and wrong?" YES! That was it. There is the light and the dark, the right and the wrong, the "Positive" and "Negative", the final two faces of truth I was missing.

So now, mixing these six truths together, does that make up the one Truth we see in existence? My Reality, Another's Reality, Knowledge, Influence, with the Positive and Negative ways we think and interact with ourselves, each other, and the world, it seems can account for everything, subjectively and objectively.

> **There is the light and the dark,**
> **the right and the wrong,**
> **the Positive and Negative.**

To demonstrate this fact just look at the world around us. We see tablets, toys, cars, cell phones, governments, nature, cultures, wars, peace, babies being born, marriage, divorce, murder, joy, sadness, etc. For example, one person enjoys one kind of activity with music, while another person hates that same activity and music. That's what it looks like when we mix these six truths together.

I looked for what has six faces/sides and yet is one, and I found a cube. Now that I unscrambled Truth and reduced it to a Cube, how was I going to see all the detail? How was I going to properly categorize these six faces of Truth?

My Reality, Another's Reality, Knowledge, Influence, with the Positive and Negative ways we think and interact with each other, ourselves, and the world, it seems can account for everything, subjectively and objectively.

One of the main observable truths in life is that everything is separate, and yet connected. So, it made sense, that I needed to find or create a pattern that could function in a way to display that truth.

But, before I talk about how I created my grid, in order to categorize all the information, I need to talk about the truth of numbers and colors.

CHAPTER 3
Truth in Numbers and Colors

Numbers and colors are what give our world height, depth, width, breadth, space, beauty, flavor, and wonder. Let's explore them together.

Numbers are their own universal language. We look around and say there are three dogs, seven cats, five trees, and if you take away one from any of those, the number cannot stay the same, regardless of what language you speak.

> **Numbers are their own universal language.**

How many suns exist in our solar system? How many fingers are on a normal hand? You may have been born with more or less appendages, or have lost them in a horrible accident, but the fact is we can count and observe the final number. Otherwise, numbers in themselves are not true, and we know from simple observation that they are.

How about when we can't see with the eyes, but can with the mind? When we speak of time, we must ask, do you mean past, present, or future? Are there more than three ways to perceive time? Some may argue that there is no past, or future, only the present. Regardless of how they argue, the three remain, what was, what is, and what will be.

Numbers are peculiar. Have you ever heard of vortex mathematics? When you start with the number one and times it by two, and then add those numbers together, you end up with a very curious loop. One times two equals two, two times two equals four, two times four equals eight, two times eight equals sixteen. Add the one and the six together you get seven, two times seven equals fourteen, add the one and the four together you get five, and two times five you get ten, add the one and the zero together you get one, then the process repeats. Also, if you go in reverse by cutting the numbers in half, the same pattern emerges.

All numbers are some combination of the foundational nine, with the zero being the oddball. I will leave that whole number to the math professor. The numbers that never appear in the loop are three, six, and nine. How are these numbers relevant in Cube Philosophy and life?

> **The numbers that never appear in the loop are three, six, and nine. How are these numbers relevant in Cube Philosophy and life?**

Let's look at some things that contain three.
There is left, right, and middle. Up, down, in-between. Forward, backward, and still. Pythagoras's three, four, five. Protons, neutrons, and electrons. X, Y, and Z axis. Knowledge, wisdom, and understanding. Right, wrong, and preference. We're even the third rock from the sun.

We humans have three cones in our eyes to perceive color: red, green, and blue. We also learned through mixing colors that there are three primary colors: blue, red, and yellow; and three secondary colors: orange, green, and purple.

Stepping aside from objectively observing colors, let's look at them through the kaleidoscope of symbolism. For instance, blue can represent trust and peace.

Red can represent love, passion, or stop. Yellow can represent light and happiness. And depending on the receptors in your eyes, one color may look like another color, and mean something unique to you.

Now let's look at some things that contain six.
A rainbow contains six main colors that are always in a specific order.

Man is a carbon-based life form, and carbon is the sixth element because of its atomic weight. According to the Hebrew scriptures God made man on the sixth day.

I believe the Truth is more complete when understood as having six faces, which made me think of a cube. Curious, Plato postulated that the element earth was made up of cubes, and modern science backs that. Baillie, Katherine. "Plato was right. Earth is made, on average, of cubes." Penn Today, July 2020.

When posing a question there are six main avenues to take, those are: who, where, when, what, why, and how. The three side streets to be more specific than "what", and "who" are: which, whose, and whom? Are we missing other words to ask questions with? No, all the variables are covered in the main six, so that the questioning process is complete.

Now let's look at nine.
Nine is the highest of the single digits. Perhaps that is why nine has been a symbolic number to many cultures, and still is to this day. Words such as complete, whole, new beginnings, wisdom, experience, the highest, and awareness have been associated with the number nine. Even the Christian scriptures mention nine fruits of the Spirit: love, joy, peace, patience, kindness, goodness, gentleness, faithfulness, and self control.

In our solar system, there are nine planets. It was only in 2006, that the ninth planet, Pluto, was redefined as a dwarf planet, aka a plutoid.

Having established the unique nature of numbers and colors, now let's take a ride in the roller-coaster to see exactly how several macro and micro multilateral three by three grids can represent the Truth we see and experience in the world.

CHAPTER 4
Shared Truth

Break out your scuba gear because this is going to be a deep dive, far away from all of us having our own Truths. By the end of this chapter, we are going to see just how much Truth we actually have in common.

Vortex mathematics shows and Nikola Tesla believed that the numbers three, six, and nine are key for obtaining a higher connection with the universe. Accordingly, I decided to divide each side of the cube into nine total sections, in other words, a three-by-three grid. Each of these boxes will have a title assigned to it. These titles relate to the different dimensions of our shared existence and represent our macro connections. Inside each box is another three-by-three grid to describe the micro connections within that macro dimension. This means on each side of the cube we get 81 squares to describe how we see ourselves, each other, and the world.

Now that the grid is in place, let's identify the nine dimensions of life we all share.

NOTE: In the following chapters every Box's Title will be Capitalized.

Every person has core values, the things which are most important to them. *Each of the nine boxes has a title and the one in the center is titled the Core box.* In the Core box there are nine squares to work with. For the moment, we are going to focus our attention on the one in the very center of the Core box. *In this square is where you will choose your fulcrum word.*

Ask yourself, what is the most important word to me in all of existence? What word means the most to me? What word does everything pivot around?

When I have asked this question, I have received such responses as love, loyalty, friendship, family, faith, hope, respect, truth, independence, and many more. I call it the fulcrum word because during construction, the fulcrum and lever are used to plumb and line a home. It's how the carpenters make a home straight and square. Some people we watch live their lives (if they were honest with themselves), have a fulcrum word such as money, sex, food, or drugs. Maybe one of these words is your current fulcrum word too, but you'd rather it wasn't.

> **I call it the fulcrum word because when constructing a house, we use the fulcrum and the lever to plumb and line the home. It is how we carpenters make the home straight and square.**

Cube philosophy helps people learn how to change. **You can redirect your life.** A new fulcrum word can help you build your life up, instead of tearing it down. Here's how...

Choose your fulcrum word!
After choosing your fulcrum word, there are eight more words to choose that mean the most to you. Four of those words will directly connect to your fulcrum word and four will indirectly connect, unless of course we started going diagonally.

Here's an example. Let's say your fulcrum word is family. Then the next four words you may want to have directly connected to family could be: provide to the left, protect to the right, love above, and respect below.

Four squares remain to fill in all the words in your Core box. You can choose these words after we talk about the eight other boxes that surround your Core box.

Now let's imagine some commonalities that could bring different peoples' truths closer to being understood by everyone.

Instead of generalizing by saying, "Well that's your truth and this is mine," just think for a moment, what are the main things all humans have in common? Do we need to eat, breathe air, and drink water? Well, yes. Does everyone get sick at some point in their lives, have emotions, or have a mind they perceive the world with? How about family, does everyone have a place they come from? If they don't know their mother or father, they still have a place of origin, right? Seeing that we have so much in common, we can title these boxes with broad terms like Consume, History, Health, and Mind.

Next, does everyone have a Personality? We know they do. To learn about how many kinds of Personalities there are, and to identify the main ones, we have an entire scientific field devoted to studying social behavior. The five main Personality types form the acronym O.C.E.A.N. to talk about those who are open, creative, extroverted, agreeable, and neurotic. We can see Personality needs to be another box.

I did some research and found that our Character is not exactly our Personality. Words like honest, hardworking, humble, lazy (for some), persistent, seeker (my personal one), or the like, are all kinds of words that you may want to put in the Character box.

The identified boxes so far are Health, History, Personality, Consume, Mind, Character, and Core, with two boxes remaining.

Paradigm would be another title word, because we each see the world through a unique pair of glasses.

In chapter one, I asked, "If we are looking at a Cube opposite each other, which side is the color orange on?" The color would be both on the right and the left, without contradicting ourselves, because perspective is the main factor that makes it so. Then perspective, or more specifically, Paradigm, would be another title word, because we each see the world through a unique pair of glasses.

For those not familiar with Dr. Covey's work, when using the word Paradigm, I am thinking of the maps we have in our Minds. Maps have meaning built into them. A map's job is to help navigate through the world. As Dr. Covey's work points out, if we have a map of Chicago, but we are in Los Angeles, we will be lost when trying to read it. Implying we should strive to have a mental map that properly aligns with how the world works. For example, when I am on a roof, I have a clear map in my Mind that tells me to be extremely cautious when I get near the edge. Maps have a specific pattern to them, and Paradigm means "example or pattern."

The final box is Paradox. Not only is Truth a Paradox, so are we. For instance, if I ask, "Are you blind?" You may say, "No, I can see just fine." Then I ask again, "Are you blind?" You may either become frustrated with me, or realize that in some ways you are blind, and in the literal sense you are not blind. This is why we have the sayings, "Do you see what I'm saying" and "Out of sight out of Mind." Ask a blind person if they are blind, they may say, "Obviously, I am blind." Ask them again if they are blind, and in some ways they know they are not. This is why we should never forget the Paradox box because we are all living paradoxes.

We should never forget the Paradox box.

Since we have now identified our nine boxes, in what order should they go on the board?

The Core, by definition, must be in the center but which of the other eight words directly relate to the Core? The way I organized the boxes is in relation to how the human body is set up. The Mind is above the Core, and Health below the Core. Don't many people say Health is in the gut, which is below the heart/Core? To me, if my Health or Mind goes, they can directly affect my Core.

I organized the boxes in relation to how the human body is set up.

The way I interact with the world is perceived through my Character and Personality, so those two go on the left and right of the Core.

On the My Reality side of the Cube, I placed the Character box on the left. I did this because by nature I am more of an analytical thinker, and that connects with my left-brain function. Also, my Personality can be Influenced through my emotions, and that is mainly a right brain function.

Now let's address the four corners that indirectly relate to the Core, but directly relate with each of the other four boxes.

It stands to reason that with the Mind is how we choose to see the world we live in. Thus, Paradigm would have to go on the left or the right of the Mind, as would the word Paradox.

Below we have the word Health in the middle, and what we Consume has a massive impact on our Health. Also, what we Consume and our Health is greatly Influenced by our History. Don't we talk about hereditary diseases and mom's home cooking? But again, does Consume go to the right or the left? We are using a three-by-three multilateral grid, which means we have to consider how the titles line up not only horizontally but vertically too.

If we were to place Consume on the left and then look at the upper two boxes, we have Character and Paradigm, or Paradox. Do you think Character relates best to Paradox or Paradigm?

I submit that Paradigm best relates to Character, because how we see the world typically has much to do with our Character, and our Character was greatly Influenced by the way we were raised, which corresponds to our History.

Therefore, instead of having Consume on the left, we see it should be History. Consume then goes on the right under Personality and Paradox. Does that work? Well, some of us eat animals and some animals eat us. We are

Consuming time and time is Consuming us. You may show us one side of your Personality, yet you can have other sides of your Personality and still be one. Both Consume and Personality are a kind of Paradox.

The completed board, from top to bottom, now reads Paradigm, Character, and History on the left. Mind, Core, and Health in the center. Finishing with Paradox, Personality, and Consume on the right. The board is set, let's see how it works.

STEP ONE: Choose your fulcrum word.
Ask yourself, what is the most important word to me? Which word does everything pivot around?

Place your fulcrum word in the middle of the Core box.

STEP TWO: Choose your center words.
Look at each box's title and ask yourself, "Which word is the most important or relevant to this part of my life?"

For example, in the center of my History box is the word present and in my Consume box is the word air/oxygen.

STEP THREE: Fill in the X-axis

The X-axis is the horizontal centerline that goes through the Character, the Core, and the Personality box.

Focus only on the Character box for the moment. The center word for your Character box represents the place of most importance or relevance in that area of your life. Now choose which two words are in the second and third places.

For example, your Character could be hopeful (if that is your center word) and also hard working, lazy, stubborn, faithful, consistent, loving, disciplined, etc.

Then finish that same process for the Core box and the Personality box.

Pause for a moment and look at the completed X-axis. How do your words relate to one another? Seeing all of them together, if you want to make a change, make it now.

STEP FOUR: Fill in the Y-axis

The Y-axis is the vertical centerline that goes through the Mind box, Core box, and the Health box.

Complete the Y-axis using the same method that was used for the X-axis.

Once you have completed steps three and four, these two centerlines make up your foundation and frame. When constructing a home, carpenters use a literal X and Y axis to find plumb (vertical) or level (horizontal). These seventeen words give your life a two-dimensional plane to work with. But that only makes up half of who you are. What you are missing is the Z axis. The Z axis is what makes this life a 3D reality.

Your frame can still lean left or right, what secures it in place are the supports, the boards that go diagonally. In the attic of a home, the gable ends are secured with a support. Two by four and two by six trusses are made up of many boards that get placed and fixed diagonally. This is done so the trusses can endure the weight of the roof, otherwise they would snap.

Don't some of us "snap" because of the pressure we are under, if we don't have proper supports in place?

Having established the value of the Z-axis (because triangulation is vital in carpentry and life) then...

STEP FIVE: Fill in both Z-axes, a.k.a. "Cross"
To fill in your Cross, use the same method that was used for the X and Y-axis.

Notice your fulcrum word is at the center of your frame and Cross. Also notice all your Core words and center words are used in these 33 words. These 33 words make up what I call, "Home." I remember when I saw my 33 words, it gave me a sense of peace, which made me feel like I was Home.

> **Notice your fulcrum word is at the center of your frame and Cross. Also notice all your Core words and center words are used in these 33 words. These 33 words make up what I call, "Home."**

STEP SIX: Fill in the two horizontal Beams

The two centerlines that are parallel to the main X-axis and contain three center words are called Beams.

Pick which words you feel best support and complement one another in those rows.

STEP SEVEN: Fill in the two vertical Trusses

The two centerlines that are parallel to the main Y-axis and contain three center words are called Trusses.

Pick which words you feel best support and complement one another in those columns.

STEP EIGHT: Fill in all the squares

Choose words that resonate with each box's title and place them in the empty squares so there are no empty boxes left.

STEP NINE: Organizing My or Another Reality

Start with the top horizontal row. Organize the words so they either compliment or balance each other out. Then repeat the process for each horizontal row. This would be a good time to triple check your X-axis.

Next is to organize each vertical column. Keep in Mind you can maintain the same words horizontally, so long as you don't move the words up or down.

I know when I did this for myself, it literally took me months. I thought at times I had it figured out. I would go back and read each horizontal and vertical line, only to find either there was a better combination, or a better word to organize each line with.

In fact, while writing this book, I discovered there was a way to make the boxes more relatable on the Reality sides of the Cube. Once I made those changes to my physical Cube, that helped me to see how to organize the other four sides. So, not only did I end up reorganizing almost all the words on all six sides of the Cube, I had to also make massive edits to this book.

My board literally mirrors your side of the board.

As mentioned, this side of the Cube is My Reality and the opposite side of the Cube is Another's Reality. What is awesome, and a bit confusing, is my side of the board literally mirrors your side of the board. Which means if I were to ask us to raise our hands in relation to the side of the board that Paradox is on, I would raise my right hand, and you would raise your left. I did this so we remember that Truth is a Paradox.

The only reason left is not right, and right is not left, but left is left, is because we agree it is. It is one of the few things we all agree upon. That's why in all countries there is a left side of the body, and a right side of the body, but when it comes to reading or driving, we disagree. English is read from left to right, and Japanese is read from right to left. Americans drive on the right side of the road, and in England they drive on the left.

To agree left could be right, and right could be left, is only a matter of perspective.

Couldn't we flip those two words, left and right (if we agreed), and not lose all the Knowledge and science we have gained? It is not like in the book 1984 when Winston is forced to believe that 2 + 2 = 5. That is a distortion of the Truth so that Big Brother could maintain control. But to agree left could be right, and right could be left, is only a matter of perspective.

Once you complete your side of the Cube, you may decide to only share it with a loved one if anyone at all. For those who are deeply honest with themselves and put a good amount of thought into organizing their board, will, in a way, have put themselves on display. Talk about a heavy first date or job interview.

If you do decide to share it with someone else, it could give you both much to think and talk about.

CHAPTER 5
Knowledge is Mainly Objective

We went deep to see our shared Realities. Now let's jump in a plane so we can get an eagle's-eye view of the vast Knowledge we have obtained over thousands of years of human history.

Questions: What are the main streams that flow into the ocean of Knowledge? What should be the name of the center box for the Knowledge side of the Cube?

I posed the later question to an old friend of mine, and he argued, "It should be the universe or God, because those are the largest and most all-encompassing ideas." "Makes sense, but we are trying to organize Knowledge, and both of those are macro ideas," I argued back, "which seems too big." "Skateboards or toys would be micro ideas, which are too small. It stands to reason that both those concepts flow better when trying to think about what is in the middle."

In the end, he didn't really agree that Homo sapiens/humans should be in the center, and I was left thinking his opinion had merit, but I felt mine did, too.

"For example, God is a religious idea, which can be one square inside the Philosophy box called religions. The universe, outer space, or the heavens, can all be taken up with one square inside of the Nature box. I think we all agree that the stars are something we see in Nature, right?" In the end, he didn't really agree that Homo sapiens/humans should be in the center, and I was left thinking his opinion had merit, but I felt mine did, too.

I pressed on and thought to myself, "Well, what we see comes out of Nature, and we can count it all." With Math we can generally or specifically measure the space between us and other objects, for instance, trees. Then we can test the integrity, durability, flexibility, and other factors to determine the object's strengths and weaknesses. We do this by adhering to a standard of measurement. Then we use the Knowledge of both the strengths and weaknesses to our advantage.

> **I pressed on and thought to myself, "Well, what we see comes out of Nature, and we can count it all."**

An example is when we build the homes we live in. The carpenter's job is not only to build the home with the lumber that came from Nature (and the mill yard), but they also need to judge each piece accordingly. Not all lumber is created equal. By looking the board over, they can observe how crowned, twisted, or bowed it is. They also need to observe how many knots are in the wood, along with taking note of the size and depth of the knots, to properly judge the board's integrity. Taking all these factors into consideration, they can accurately choose the place it is best suited for. The carpenter accomplishes this task utilizing Math.

Math is all around and inside us, but math/numbers, are not colors.

As we learned in chapter three, colors are objective, but also subjective. Colors dance with our emotions. Just as when watching an old black and white film, it emits a different vibe than when it's in color. Color adds flavor and variety. Nature creates color. But then I realized that we also have the saying, "Nature didn't make those." So, how do I account for everything Nature didn't make?

So, how do I account for everything Nature didn't make?

With this line of thinking, I thought maybe the Arts could go in the middle, instead of Nature, because well, "We did make those." In the Arts box I could put words like music, literature, dance, theater, and art.

My Mind and heart just didn't feel that was right because what about the numbers? Sure, we make music with numbers, but how each individual feels about those notes and their timing are so subjective.

Yes, the Arts are literally objective because they were created and exist to this day, but how do I account for how we think and feel about them?

I thought maybe Science could be the center box.

Then I thought maybe Science could be the center box, because it encompasses colors, numbers, and how we think and feel. In that box, I could put words like astronomy, geology, physics, computers, and social. That could account for much, but then how does that align with History?

Arguably Science has accumulated over time, which is a part of History. The great thing about true Science though, is its ability to stay neutral and only search for hard facts...but wait, that is something we humans are actively doing. Seeking to discover and disprove, to refine and build, for the greater good and for future generations.

> **How we humans created the art and practice of Science is said to have been born from Philosophy.**

How we humans created the art and practice of Science is said to have been born from Philosophy. Philosophy in Greek means "The love of wisdom." We humans learned that by observing repeated actions that have a consistent result is something we could use to our advantage. That to me is wise, plain and simple. As a matter of fact, in Latin, Homosapien means "wise man." What kept coming back to my Mind was that Homo sapiens should be at the root of Knowledge because we are the creators of Philosophy, which in turn created the art of discovering Science.

Therefore, I concluded that Homo sapiens should be in the middle. I tried it, and it worked, because the Arts could go in the Homosapiens box. Then we can easily discuss History, Philosophy, Nature, Science, and more.

I concluded that Homo sapiens should be in the middle.

Now that I had thought through which box goes in the center, I wanted to finish identifying the eight that surround it, but I was having a difficult time.

I was on a trip with my friends headed to Seattle, Washington, to skate at Pattison's West. On the drive I kept playing with this side of the cube by writing in my journal different words I thought could work.

After talking with a few different people, I finally decided that Science, Health, History, Math, Philosophy, Technology, Nature, Homo sapiens, and the Unknown all had to be titles for the individual boxes. Next was how to organize them.

First, I organized them vertically. I realized Science, Math, and Philosophy are the methods we use. History, Homo sapiens, and Technology are the things we create. The Unknown, Nature, and Health are the things we try to investigate and/or manipulate. Then it was time to organize the words horizontally.

The finished board, from the left to right, starting across the top, now reads Nature, Technology, and Science. Why?

Science studies Nature to learn about the laws and resources there are, so we can make the Technology we create.

The middle is Unknown, Homo sapiens, and Philosophy. Why?

We Homo sapiens use Philosophy to think about the Unknown and seek to discover it. Also, Philosophy is where the ideas of God, astrology, chaos vs order, laws, and more come out of. These thoughts gave birth to much of the music, art, and stories that have been around for thousands of years or more.

The bottom row is Health, History, and Math. Why?

Not only have these topics evolved over time, but the study of time/History is literally counting, which is Math. Also, how long we live as a species, to be a part of History, is in direct relation to our Health.

To see why Technology is a box's title, let's look at the nine words I placed in there.

To see why Technology is a box's title, let's look at the nine words I placed in there. They are audio, optics, navigation, transportation, construction, tools, communication, machines, and automation. It was easier to come up with these words because of how they relate to the Homo sapiens box below.

For instance, we humans hear audio, see optics, move navigation plus transportation, build construction plus tools, speak communication, and live by using machines plus automation.

Under each of these nine words, we can make subcategories. For example, under transportation we can have planes, trains, automobiles, submarines, boats, motorcycles, skates, rockets, etc.

> **Under each of these nine words, we can make subcategories.**

The sheer amount of time it would take to talk about all the words I think go in each box would make this book extra-long, and I prefer to keep it short. Plus, with so many Minds looking at this Cube together, I bet we can make it far more refined than what I currently have.

Admittedly, I don't know if this side of the Cube could ever contain all the wealth of human Knowledge in just 81 words. As far as I know, this is only a starting point to have a simple platform that is easy to work with.

With so many Minds looking at this Cube together, I bet we can make it far more refined than what I currently have.

What I hope I have shown is that Knowledge is mainly objective, because we see or know about the events, ideas, and objects that exist in our world.

The only two boxes that are mostly subjective are History and Philosophy.

History is a matter of your perspective mixed with the objective artifacts, architecture, and records that help to narrow down what happened.

Philosophy contains the word religions. Knowing how many religions are in the world, we know it is a highly subjective subject. Yet, we can read their writings and learn about their doctrines, which is an objective fact.

What I hope I have shown is that Knowledge is mainly objective,

because we see or know about the events, ideas, and objects that exist in our world.

Now we have seen the Knowledge that we use, and the Knowledge that is (reference chapter 2), on this side of the Cube. How about we mosey on over to the opposite side, to see how our Realities Influence the Truth, and in turn, how the Truth Influences our Realities.

CHAPTER 6
Influence is Mainly Subjective

We have seen the depths and the heights of Truth. Now let's see how far we can open our Minds to try and grasp the expanse of Truth.

We have all heard it said, "Beauty is in the eye of the beholder." That statement is true and highly subjective. That is how Influence works, what is beautiful to one is plain or disgusting to another. How about the saying, "What is one man's medicine is another man's poison." How do some get sick so easily and others don't? The numerous factors that Influence us humans are very subjective, and objective, which is why the Truth is so elusive. Especially when we try to think that we are all the same… and we aren't.

> **"Beauty is in the eye of the beholder." That statement is true and highly subjective. That is how Influence works, what is beautiful to one is plain or disgusting to another.**

Each human being, though they have much in common with each other, is unique. Just think of how a vegetarian diet works for some and not for others. How one lifestyle can make some thrive and that same lifestyle is extremely depressing to someone else.

Using the same grid as the other faces, let's identify the areas of life that have the most significant Influence on us.

We all went through a massive shift in 2020 (I find it ironic that normal vision is 20/20, and I've heard many people say they had their eyes opened in 2020, curious). One of the main factors that made that shift possible was the fear most of us felt. It seemed our Emotions were at the helm during that time. I know mine were. *This is why I believe Emotions are the core of Influence.*

I believe Emotions are the core of Influence.

This becomes even more apparent when we observe the life of Dr. Victor Frankl. Dr. Frankl was an Austrian who earned a doctorate in Medicine in 1931. He worked as a psychiatrist, until he and his family were forced to endure the Holocaust. After that awful and tragic phase of his life, in 1948 he earned his second doctorate in Philosophy. Later he founded Logotherapy and Existential analysis. Logotherapy was created to help people find meaning and purpose in their life.

> **The example Dr. Frankl left us is to search for the light in the darkness and find our purpose for living.**

Think about how Dr. Frankl felt during those years. I'm sure during those very dark moments, it felt impossible at times to find a reason to keep on going. I can imagine he asked himself,

"What's the meaning of it all?"

To see how his pain and suffering Influenced him is truly amazing. He didn't become bitter, vengeful, or defeated. Instead, he chose to glean the beautiful and weighty lessons that came from those Negative experiences. Then he passed those teachings on to others.

The example Dr. Frankl left us is to search for the light in the darkness and find our purpose for living.

So, with Emotions at the center of the grid, let's think about what directly plays upon our Emotions.

Just as it is said, "Beauty is in the eye of the beholder." Then what we see, smell, hear, taste, and touch are experiences that directly affect our Emotions. Let's title a box Senses.

How about if someone is aggressive, kind, calm, lazy, or funny. Does that affect our Emotions? Certainly. Then Behavior must be a box.

The Environment we experience can affect our Emotions. "Why aren't you going outside today?" Response, "There's a blizzard." "How come you don't feel safe traveling to that place?" "Because they're in the middle of a war and people are dying, it's chaotic." Also, without our Environment we literally die, so it needs to be a box that directly connects.

Another area of life that Influences us is during a business meeting, when we go to school, or when we are alone. All these kinds of Interactions (or lack thereof) directly affect our Emotions.

There are several ways in which to organize the words Senses, Behavior, Interactions, and Environment around the Emotions box.

The way I organized it was Behavior below Emotions, and Environment above Emotions. Why? Because some people say, since it is a rainy day (Environment), they feel kind of sad (Emotion), and then they act depressed (Behavior). That's why I placed those three boxes in that order.

> **There are many ways to organize the words Senses, Behavior, Interactions, and Environment around Emotions.**

Next, I placed Senses to the right, with Interactions on the left. How about when we walk into a church to witness a ceremony (Interaction), and we hear (Senses) the two people exchange vows. Witnessing these kinds of moments can affect how we feel (Emotions). Speaking of the Interactions we experience in life, I think we should add the sixth sense to one of the squares in the Senses box. I believe some phenomena in the universe are better understood in six. Also, some people claim to understand and know how to use their sixth sense. Regardless, we need to have nine words to fill up the Senses box, and only five are obvious. Other words I used were invisible and opposite. Invisible includes subcategory words such as spiritual or ESP. For opposites the subcategory words are pain and pleasure, hot and cold, etc., etc. Why? Because opposites are subjective as well as objective contrasting sensations. For example, why does one person like it between 70 to 72 degrees in the home, and some crazy people like it between 60 to 65? Brrr.

Now that the four boxes that directly connect to Emotions have been named, let's find out what indirectly connects.

Focusing on the upper right corner, which two words are directly connected? They are Environment and

Senses. What is the best word we can think of that correlates with those? I believe it is Nature. Nature can have words in it such as cycles, death, sun, moon, earth, and animals. An example of how these three can work in unison is the sun (Nature), could account for it being hot (Environment), which is something that touches (Sensation) us humans.

With Nature to the right of the Environment box, what word can work on the left?

What has the greatest impact on our Environment as well as the Natural world?

How did we all feel when our governments told us to stay in our homes to avoid a wandering virus? How about when mom and dad put up a Christmas tree, and the smell of potpourri permeates the home? If we are in a business setting, don't we talk about the work Environment?

Governments, families, and businesses are all kinds of Institutions. These Institutions have a direct impact on our shared Environment and Nature.

Institutions are now above the Interactions box. That makes sense, right? We talk with our coworkers, mom and dad, people from church, or listen to the media. All these kinds of Interactions occur because of our shared Institutions.

Institutions have a direct impact on our shared Environment and Nature.

The lower left corner has the words Interactions above it, and Behavior to the right of it. Also, take into consideration that Institutions are above Interactions. When we think of politicians, teachers, policemen, and investors, who either work for or own those Institutions, what do they all have in common? Aren't they all kinds of Influencers?

Whether we Interact with the Influencers by being in their presence, listening to them, or watching them on TV, they have the potential to change our Behavior. This is especially true when we are in the presence of an enforcer (Influencer) who looks and acts the part. Keep in Mind, the Senses box is directly across from

Interactions. It mixes with our Emotions, as we listen to the Influencers, who come from our shared Institutions.

Whether we Interact with Influencers by being in their presence, listening to them, or watching them on TV, they have the potential to change our Behavior.

There are four words that directly connect, which means we must account for them when trying to solve the final box, in the lower right corner. Let's take a look. They are Influencers, Behavior, Nature, and Senses.

Part of Nature is that things die. Because of that we instinctually feel the need to pass on our genes as well as seek shelter to get out of the elements. We do both actions to survive.

Think about how our societies are set up to combat or work in harmony with Nature. How do we get the masses and ourselves to go in a specific direction or perform a certain kind of action? What is it that we see in our Minds' eye, that is Influencing how we move? These objects and/or ideas are generally referred to as Incentives and/or Deterrents. One to represent the Positive, and one to represent the Negative.

The Incentive to go to school is to gain Knowledge by listening to the teacher who is an Influencer. How well we listen has a lot to do with their Behavior and ours. The Incentive to work a job or run a business is to earn money so we can have food, shelter, power, and many other things. Some people get lost in the Incentive box because of drugs, money, sex, or status.

As for the obvious Deterrent, which is death, not a whole lot needs to be said. I say that because we know for many people there are worse things than death. Torture, in all its various forms, can be worse than death. Stepping aside from those extreme Deterrents there are walls, doors, odors, penalties, music, art, etc.

> **What is it that we see in our Minds' eye, that is Influencing how we move? These objects and/or ideas are generally referred to as**

Incentives and/or Deterrents.

Incentives & Deterrents absolutely affect our Emotions. They are the final box on the Influence side of the Cube.

Now that all nine boxes have been identified on the Influence side of the Cube, let's read them from left to right in descending order.

They are Institutions, Environment, Nature, Interactions, Emotions, Senses, Influencers, Behavior, and Incentives & Deterrents.

These are the main things I can see that have the greatest Influence on all our lives.

Having revealed four sides of the Cube, with all these boxes and squares, it may be a bit confusing.

The easiest way to remember how to organize these four sides of the Cube is to imagine you and a friend are on a hike. While on this hike you come across a Cube that is six feet tall, wide, and thick. You and your friend stand on opposite sides of this Cube. You, dear reader, the side facing you would be My Reality. The side facing your friend is Another's Reality. To your friend's left, but on your right, is Knowledge, and on the opposite side of Knowledge is Influence.

How to organize these four sides is to imagine you and a friend are on a hike. While on this hike you come across a Cube that is six feet tall, wide, and thick.

Looking at these four faces allows us to see why discovering the Truth is simple, and yet complex.

Before we move on, let's finish the hike analogy, since it leads us perfectly into the next chapter.

As you and your friend are looking at this Cube, it would be very easy to think of it as having a dark side, right? It's on the ground. Knowing there is a dark side, we can also see, and say, there is a light side, because one side is facing up towards the sky.

As you and your friend are looking at this Cube, it would be very easy to think of it as having a dark side, right? It's on the ground.

In the next chapter, we are going to follow Alice down the rabbit hole (which just so happens to go under the Cube) to see the Positive (light) and Negative (dark) ways we interact with the world, each other, and ourselves. All while trying to keep in Mind the four faces of this small and yet immense Cube.

CHAPTER 7
The Quest for the Optimal Shared Truth

Brace yourselves, this is going to be the longest and heaviest chapter that will pull on all our heart strings. Keep in Mind, we are prone to get lost when we wander off into darkness, and we are going down the rabbit hole, where no light can enter in.

> **To experience true light, we must know real darkness. It can't remain out of sight out of Mind, otherwise we are bound to trip over it.**

Therefore, I ask that you please guard your hearts with this beautiful quote, "If it were not for the backdrop of night, we would not see the myriad of stars." To experience true light, we must know real darkness. It can't remain out of sight out of Mind, otherwise we are bound to trip over it, because it most certainly is there, even if we are refusing to acknowledge it.

One of the main Emotions that blinds us is fear. Let me tell you a true story that demonstrates this fact.

I had taken on a new job working in North Dakota, trying to see if I could make enough money in the oil fields. I had been gone for about thirty days and was back in town for only four. It was the third night, so my wife and I were getting ready for bed. I knew our four-year-old son Gabriel was asleep in his bed, but I started to hear a knocking sound coming from his room. I went into his room, turned on the light, but the light bulb burnt out. I turned on the hall light, and then went back into his dim room to see what was making that sound. As I looked around, I couldn't see anything obvious, so I made my way to him. I noticed his body was moving, and then I realized he was the one making that knocking sound. I assumed he was having a bad dream. When I turned him towards me, I started to feel like something was wrong.

> **One of the main Emotions that blinds us is fear.**

I shook him a few times, but he wasn't waking up, and it appeared only one side of his body was moving. I moved enough so the light from the hallway shined on his face and an extreme amount of drool came pouring out of his mouth. I immediately yelled for my wife who was in the bathroom. I said, "Hey, something is wrong with Gabriel, he's not responding and there's a lot of drool!" I had been through first aid training, which meant I had learned about seizures, but this was my first time really seeing one firsthand, and it was my son.

Fortunately, my wife knew what to do. We got him out into the living room, turned him on his side, and she told me to call 911. The firemen arrived within minutes (because there is a fire station less than a mile away). My son was still on the floor, his right side was limp with the left side periodically flailing about. As soon as I heard, and then saw their truck, I ran outside "My son, my son, please help my son!" The firemen knew how to keep him safe until the paramedics could get there. Once the paramedics arrived, they gave him a shot which calmed his body, and then informed us our son had just experienced a grand mal seizure.

They informed us our son just experienced a grand mal seizure.

As soon as Gabriel was stable, they got him on a stretcher and into the back of an ambulance. We followed him to the hospital where we met with a doctor who told us what to expect. I had one day left in town and was scheduled to get on the train the next morning at 1:30 a.m. to head back to North Dakota. We were already struggling financially. My wife couldn't work because our boy was sick so often, which meant the entire financial burden fell on me. I reluctantly left my family so we wouldn't lose our home.

While I was back trying to work, my Mind kept returning to my son. A few days into my twelve-day shift, we found out we were going to lose the insurance through the state because my new job made too much money. When I factored in paying for insurance with travel expenses, the money wasn't adding up. I had an accident on the job (I think in part because of the chaotic state I was in) and was terminated at the end of the twelve days.

> **Upon returning home, not only was I dealing with figuring out how to pay for everything now, but my son was also shying away from me. He didn't remember who I was.**

Upon returning home, not only was I dealing with figuring out how to pay for everything now, but my son was also shying away from me. He didn't remember who I was. Sadly, that can be a side effect of having nocturnal seizures, they disrupt the "download process" when you're sleeping. Then you lose not only that day of information, but sometimes weeks before. After learning about this from the doctor, it made more sense why our son would be able to perform typical functions, like pick up his sippy cup for a week, and then forget how the next. I'm sharing this so we can see how powerful our Emotions are and to show we don't think well when we allow them to overtake us.

> **I'm sharing this so we can see how powerful our Emotions are, and to show we don't think well when we allow them to overtake us.**

Looking back, had I not allowed my Emotions to overwhelm me, I would have been able to think clearer. That way I could have helped my son, avoided the accident, and made better choices during that time. However, isn't that life? We learn as we grow and experience different scenarios, assuming we are willing to look back and glean the lessons from those dark moments. Isn't that what wisdom is, to learn from our mistakes as well as others so we can make wiser decisions in the future? I think yes. Life is a roller-coaster with ups, downs, loops, twists, and turns. Hopefully, at every turn we learn something new without forgetting the old.

So now, how do we take this Knowledge and apply it? When you voted recently were you thinking or feeling? How about when you got into that argument with your partner or boss? How many of our convictions are based solely on our feelings? I am not saying that our feelings are wrong, I am simply pointing out that they are powerful and can create strong biases that blind us.

> **So now, how do we take this Knowledge and apply it?**

When Alice followed the white rabbit down the hole, she wandered off into Wonderland. Why did she go there? Wasn't it because she felt her sister was trying to control her? But Wonderland is a made-up world, devoid of the Truth. When Alice came back, then she could see how her sister was trying to help her grow, not control her. Alice's unchecked Emotions, which gave birth to her stubbornness, are what were keeping her from the optimal way of living in the real world.

Many things in life are a double edge sword. Emotions are beautiful and empowering, but they can also be grotesque and debilitating. Our imaginations are great when they are reigned in with a purpose, otherwise we wander off into Wonderland.

Question: *What is the best way for us to engage in this complex life?* For instance, if I give you fifty dollars, did I just help you or did I just enable you? The action looks the same, but one is Positive, and one is Negative. When two men fight to test their skills, like in the MMA, what separates those actions from actual war or a street fight? Which is Positive and which is Negative, is in the details, and those details have to do with the heart.

What is our aim and motivation?

When we confined ourselves to avoid sickness and potential death, what problems did we create because of that? If you have attached yourself with Emotion to a virus, then my words right now are most likely falling on deaf ears. Maybe you are consumed with fear and refusing to see it is not as simple as what you feel. We must take into consideration the four sides of the Cube, while we search for the best answers to the Positive and Negative ways that we interact with one Another.

> **Many things in life are a double edge sword.**

Seeing how difficult it is, searching for the optimal way to share this world, let me try and simplify it a bit. Let's think of ourselves as numbers for a moment. How can a three tell a five how to live? Can a three or five know what it's like to be a two or a seven? What do a one and a nine have in common? They are all numbers, but not the same.

Now imagine the Positive face of the Cube represents the best way of living together and the Negative face represents the worst. You're a seven, and you think you should put the seven in the middle as your fulcrum word. I am a five, and I think I should put the five in the middle as my fulcrum word. Seems fine, but then when we talk about how we are going to share this world, will either one of us truly understand where the other is coming from? Is it even a possibility to arrive at the Positive way to live in harmony, accounting for all our differences, if we each have our own numbers in the center? What if the one, two, three, five, seven, and nine were to agree to place the eight in the middle?

The "8" is a unique number. Many of us know it to be the infinity symbol, not just a number. If all of us agreed that the number eight should be in the center, then even with so much diversity we could still get much closer to how we solve the puzzle of an optimal shared existence.

> **Imagine the Positive face of the Cube represents the best way of living together, and the Negative face represents the worst.**

Before we continue any further, I fully admit, I don't know what the optimal way of living together is, I only have my opinion. That's why this Chapter is titled "The Quest for the Optimal Shared Truth."

*It will be a journey, and one I hope
we are on together.*

I do know, though, that even if we discover all possible Science, have no mystery left to uncover, and have not yet learned to have genuine affection for Another's entire being (because we are all born with intrinsic value), it will all have been for nothing. Think about actors playing a role. They can demonstrate love, even feel the Emotion to appear as one with it, but it's still fiction, and we need genuine love working in tolerance to thrive.

Having stated that I don't know, here's the best I could come up with to name all the boxes for the Positive and Negative faces of the Cube.

To start, the Positive and the Negative mirror one another with only one difference. That is, I placed

Wisdom on the Positive side in the upper right corner, and Foolishness on the Negative side in the upper left corner. I simply can't see how not learning from our mistakes, and not learning how to genuinely listen, and not learning how to communicate effectively, will ever be Positive. We would have never progressed as far as we have if we never learned to evolve our Minds and therefore our actions. Think about what our world would look like if cannibalism never died out...

The Positive and the Negative mirror one another, with only one difference.

From here, knowing that the Positive and Negative faces mirror each other, I am going to only discuss the boxes from the Positive point of view. That way I don't need to be uselessly redundant in using left and right.

When we think about why our societies survive, it seems it's because there is a set of Core Values that we agree upon.

When you're on the job, how does it feel when your boss doesn't communicate with you? Or, if they do talk to you, they seem smug and condescending? How about from your boss's point of view when you're showing up late to work, and have a rotten attitude? They're upset because they want you to fulfill the role they're paying you for. How about when decisions are made at home without you knowing?

Proper communication is vital.

> **Why our societies survive, it seems it's because there is a set of Core Values that we agree upon.**

If we agree to share and abide by a common set of Core Values, we can go far. Words that would sustain an optimal society would be communication, honesty, accountability, integrity, discernment, and discipline. If we all chose to live with these words in Mind, we could have a well knitted and thriving society.

The Negative side of the board also has Core Values, only the words are different. Selfishness, envy, greed, deception, sloth, or words of that nature go in the center. Do I really need to elaborate why the Negative side won't work? I think it is self-evident.

With Core Values in the center, let's start to identify the other eight boxes.

Societies are made up of different People Groups. Let's place People Groups to the right. People Groups could include words like self, friends, state, nation, or world.

Those People fill up society's Institutions. Institutions to the left of Core Values would have words such as governments, religion, entertainment, family, business, and health care. Ideally, those groups of People in our shared Institutions would operate with Positive Core Values in Mind, instead of the Negative ones.

Above Core Values would be Consume and below would be Environment, because without either one of these two boxes, we die. Therefore, all Positive and Negative interactions between People Groups take place in a shared Environment.

All Positive and Negative interactions between People Groups take place in a shared Environment.

On the Influence side, Environment is a box above Emotions. On the Positive side of the Cube, we are going to place the Environment box below Core Values. This lets us remember that our Environment is above, below, and all around us, all the time.

If we are seeking to act in a way that wisely harmonizes with our Environment, this will require a set of Core Values. Striving to agree upon a set of Core Values is challenging due to our strong Emotional attachments. When we don't keep our Emotions in check, we quickly lose unity. Therefore, we need to make certain shifts that aim to minimize suffering in all directions.

Any shift in how we treat our Environment, greatly affects what we Consume.

Consume would have to be a box, because without it, we die.

Consume would have to be a box because without it, we die. It's an absolute law in our universe. It's why we have laws that prohibit us from mixing our waste with our water sources. What we choose to Consume is something we should talk about. Discussing the most Positive ways to Consume include the practices of how we produce and care for our food, particularly livestock.

Having identified the titles for the four boxes that directly connect to Core Values, let's address the four corners.

I already stated that Wisdom is in the upper right corner. That means People Groups is being flanked by Core Values and Wisdom. With those in Mind, what word is the most logical conclusion for the bottom right corner? I think the word is Beliefs. Don't many of us ask: "What do I believe in?" "Is what I'm believing in wise?" "What values does it teach me?"

> **Don't many of us ask:**
> **"What do I believe in?"**
> **"Is what I'm believing in wise?"**
> **"What values does it teach me?"**

Negative Beliefs don't require Wisdom, only Foolishness. Though, make no mistake, the Negative face has its Beliefs. Beliefs go in the lower right corner.

Environment is now to the left of Beliefs. How we Interact with our Environment is a direct result of what we Believe about it, and ourselves.

So far, we have identified two columns. Looking at both from top to bottom, starting in the middle is Consume, Core-Values, and Environment. The three to the right are Wisdom, People Groups, and Beliefs. The only identified word on the left is Institutions in the center. How are we going to deduce what words should be above and below Institutions?

When playing certain games, sometimes the only way to solve which number goes in a particular box is by searching for the numbers that can't go in that box. Paradox? To explain this Paradox, is Edison's quote, "I have not failed 10,000 times. I've successfully found 10,000 ways that will not work."

When playing certain games, sometimes the only way to solve which number goes in a particular box is by searching for the numbers that can't go in that box, Paradox?

We know the words that directly connect to the lower left corner are Institutions, Environment, and Beliefs. The words that directly connect to the upper left corner are Institutions, Consume, and Wisdom. These words are what we need to consider when trying to identify the best words that can contain the meaning of those unnamed spaces.

In chapter six, two identified boxes were Environment and Institutions. These two boxes are on the Influence side of the Cube. What we must also keep in Mind though, is that there is only one Cube, in Cube Philosophy, and it represents one complex Truth. So, when I say that I see the words Environment and Institutions as more concrete ideas, I am relating to them with my Knowledge, not my Emotions. Beliefs are more of an Emotional response, and that does relate with the Influence side of the Cube, because Emotions are the core of Influence. This means we have a two to one ratio, two for Knowledge, and one for Influence. The Influence in this case though is, Beliefs. Wow! With so many religions, ideas, opinions, concepts, and multiplication of words, what is the right answer?

Back to that in a moment.

What if we reduced all the religions down, and tried to sum them up in one word? What could that word be?

What I enjoy about Cube Philosophy is we all get to choose our own eight unique words to place in our own Core box, in a variety of combinations, while having the possibility of agreeing to be united around one word.

To have billions united around one word, what would our world look like?

Back to the discussion.

Influence could be summed up as cause and effect; it is a fundamental truth we all know. Beliefs have to do with why and how we feel about choosing to affect something. To Believe we need to Behave in a specific way, to achieve consistent Positive results, means we would have to have set Protocols for our Institutions and People Groups to follow.

Protocols are a kind of Knowledge we create for everyone to obey/use, and we had a two to one ratio in favor of Knowledge. So instead of Cause and Effect in the lower left corner, it seems Protocols is better. If anyone does not adhere to our agreed upon Protocols our elected officials who run our Institutions would administer justice.

> **To Believe we need to Behave in a specific way, to achieve consistent Positive results, means we would have to have set Protocols for our Institutions and People Groups to follow.**

Justice is the idea of Law and Order, and their symbol is the scales/Libra. The scales symbolize our actions throughout life and remind us of the effects we have caused. The scales also symbolically say there might be some Checks we have to cash, to Balance things out in the end. Instead of Cause and Effect for the upper left corner, let's go with Checks & Balances, and this is the final box.

With this, every box's title on all six sides of the Cube has been uncovered.

Checks and Balances can be Positive or Negative. In a corrupt society, those at the top have their forms of Checks and Balances, which is if you step out of line they wrongfully punish or kill you, right? In an altruistic society, the officials use Knowledge with Wisdom to administer fair and just verdicts instead. But what if the officials don't choose to follow the Protocols? What kinds of Checks would they have to cash, to Balance things out?

> **Instead of Cause and Effect for the upper left corner, let's go with Checks & Balances, and this is the final box.**

So now, starting on the left side and reading from top to bottom, the board is as follows: Checks & Balances, Institutions, and Protocols. Consume, Core Values, and Environment. Finished with Wisdom (or Foolishness), People Groups, and Beliefs.

The board is set, now we get to discuss what goes in the squares in each box, or if the name of a box needs to change all together. What makes this Cube unique is we get to see how each word relates to all the other words, without having to hold an entire conversation in our Minds.

In the next chapter, I will sum up Cube Philosophy and how it can be used in daily life. I will also talk about the physical Cube I made, and how I used it to help me learn more about myself, others, and the world in which I live.

CHAPTER 8
Please Take the Paradox Pill

"Think outside the box, by thinking on the box"

Cube Philosophy grew out of my desire to know the Truth. I have declared, "I don't care if I go to hell (assuming that is a real place) as long as the Truth comes forward." I know I can't fully find it on my own and that is why I have taught myself to really listen. Which basically means I learned how (with great struggle and pain) to keep my Emotions in check so I could properly value each individual voice. Something that helped me become a good listener was reading the poem Desiderata almost daily for a year and committing it to memory. If you don't know that poem, I highly recommend reading it.

We humans are an amazing species. I, for one, am very grateful to be a part of us, because we can have some of the most fascinating and inspiring conversations with each other, which can lead to some incredible synergy.

Cube Philosophy was created to help facilitate deeper and more meaningful conversations. Before you use Cube Philosophy, let's go over the rules.

Rules for Cube Philosophy

RULE NUMBER 1

Terminology is Key

If we can't agree a cube is basically a box that has six sides, the conversation will be pointless.

RULE NUMBER 2

There is Only One Cube

There is one Truth we are seeking to understand. My Reality, Another's Reality, Knowledge, Influence, with the Positive and Negative ways we interact are the main variables that make up the one shared Cube/Truth.

RULE NUMBER 3

Cube Philosophy is Not a Religion

Cube Philosophy is just that, a Philosophy. It's a way of thinking that I Believe can help us connect with ourselves, others, and the world.

RULE NUMBER 4
Cube Philosophy is a Journey

No one has arrived; All Realities have the potential to learn and evolve.

RULE NUMBER 5
Cube Philosophy Provides Orientation

When Interacting with Another Reality, I know My Reality can potentially pass on Knowledge and/or Influence, in a Positive and/or Negative way.

CUBE PHILOSOPHY BELIEFS

- Each individual voice adds to this world, and we can learn from all of them.
- Each individual has specific value and talents they can cultivate.
- Each individual body, Mind, and heart is unique.
- The greatest joy is to unravel the mystery that is one's self, in light of the collective, in order to gain a sense of purpose and destiny.

Cube Philosophy is used in real time.

One way Cube Philosophy can be utilized is during a discussion about life. This could involve an event, or when trying to solve how you want to operate your home. This simple and yet complex Cube enables both parties to see how interwoven each word and concept is to one another. It also allows both parties to see in real time where the other is coming from.

Another way Cube Philosophy is used in real time is when an individual is managing a vital role in society. They can feel confident in that role because they have the Mind, Personality, and Character that can handle all the responsibilities that come with that position. Which means when they are performing well, they should be rewarded for it. Because that individual has taken the time to become competent by obtaining the Knowledge and Influence needed to perform in that specific role efficiently and effectively.

Once you know the entire Cube by heart, it allows you to quickly see what you are proficient or inept at.

A third way Cube Philosophy is used in real time. This Philosophy knows some people are not as pivotal, relatively speaking, yet they are still a part of the whole. If we were thinking in terms of our physical bodies, to some areas we ascribe more value, and others not as much. Still, no matter where we get cut, burned, or sustain an injury, it affects the whole. True, with the Mind we can ignore the pain, but the fact is we can look and observe that some part of the body is not in its optimal condition.

To illustrate what I mean by each person having value, let's look at my handicapped son Gabriel. In practical matters, how can he contribute to society? He is 16 and still in diapers. He can't understand many things because he has an IQ around 50. So, what is his value?

> **To illustrate what I mean by each person having value, let's look at my handicapped son, Gabriel. In practical matters, how can he contribute to society?**

Before I got to see what his value was, and is, I had to figure out myself first. That was a difficult process. It took me years to retrace my self-talk and actions, to arrive at the truth of who I was.

Using specific indicators/markers, I was able to see that when I was younger, I was not only arrogant, but self-absorbed with my expectations, too. Becoming aware of the powerful bias my expectations gave me showed me I wasn't then the dad Gabriel deserved to have. I was living a Positive and Negative existence at the same time, how? Because no one is all Positive or all Negative. As I discussed in chapter seven, the action of giving someone fifty dollars could be Positive or Negative, which is why it is difficult to know what kind of action just took place.

To get at the roots of my actions with my son, I had to ask myself a direct and weighty question. "Was Gabriel the son I wanted?" The brutal and true answer back then was, unfortunately, "No." Fortunately, the truth for the last several years is, "He isn't the son I originally wanted, but he is the son I needed, which makes him the son I do want now." I am so grateful that the universe/

God gave me my son to look after and love. To me he is a pivotal and vital part of my life.

I believe his value is in simply being his funny, innocent self, and that gives me the opportunity to be the best version of myself. Being Gabriel's father is continually teaching me to lay down my expectations and accept what is. From where I'm standing today, it is far better than anything I could have ever possibly envisioned with my limited finite Mind.

> **I believe his value is in simply being his funny, innocent self, and that gives me the opportunity to be the best version of myself.**

We never know who will Influence us for better or worse. Who will say the words or perform the actions that send us down a particular path. It seems for most it's our family and friends. This is why we say to each other, "Choose your friends wisely."

I have been thinking about this Cube for over a decade. After having shared my idea with John Ward, at the beginning of 2022, he told me I should write a book. I did write this book, but before I did, I made a physical working cube. I fabricated it out of sheet metal from the shop dumpster (I asked) and then went down to Hobby Lobby® and bought a bunch of sheets of magnets. You know? The ones we use for photos that we put on the fridge. I cut them up into squares and started writing words on them. It took me a few months to organize the My Reality side of the Cube. For a little time, I almost forgot I made this Cube originally for myself, I got so caught up with the project. One day I came home from work and realized I needed to use my Cube to see if it really works. I can say anecdotally that it did.

I have been thinking about this Cube for over a decade.

Seeing my eighty-one words and organizing them has given me a greater sense of self-awareness.

I also identified roughly sixty-one words that we all have in common, which helped me learn much about others as well.

Now I feel it is ready to share with the world, to see if it can help you too. I shared it with two friends who are super close to each other. When they switched sides, the reaction was funny. "Ohhh, that's you!" You can learn so much about others, yourself, and the world by using the Connection Cube.

The Connection Cube has much symbolism to help us remember. I did this by utilizing the three primary and three secondary colors.

My Reality is Blue. You may ask, "Why not Red, Yellow, or any other color?" Well, because Blue is my favorite color and I have always aspired to be a Blue flame. Plus, it's my Cube. Also, don't we humans say we are either Blue blood (royalty) or Red blood (commoners)? In the political sphere, Democrats are Blue and Republicans are Red. Dallas Cowboys vs the 49ers. Crips and the Bloods. Vampires and humans.

> **The Connection Cube has much symbolism to help us remember. I did this by utilizing three primary and three secondary colors.**

Perhaps that has been a common theme because when we look at the veins through our skin, they look Blue, but we all bleed Red. Red is for Another's Reality. Blue and Red are primary, and so are we.

What happens when I want it my way, and you want it your way, don't we end up with the worst way? Purple then is for the Negative side, because when we mix Blue and Red, we get Purple. I do know that when we typically see Purple we think of royalty, spirituality, or God. But then, how many atrocities have been committed in the name of God and King? Also, that guy was being a royal pain in the... That is why Purple, to me, can represent the Negative.

When we both submit to a better way, we end up with the Positive way, which is Yellow, the third primary color. In Cube Philosophy (and life), Yellow symbolizes joy, light, energy, friendship, imagination, optimal, and the sun. The sun is above all Realities; hence the Positive (Yellow) side of the cube is on top.

When we mix the Positive Yellow with My Reality Blue, we end up with Green. One saying we have is that a person is Green with envy. Nature is also Green, and some of us have Green thumbs to Influence Nature with. That is why Green reminds me of Influence.

When we mix Another's Reality Red with the Positive Yellow, we get Orange. That is what happens when we use our Minds in a Positive way, we obtain Knowledge. Orange reminds me of discovering objective Knowledge because oranges are Orange.

In closing, I must tell you I debated heavily with myself if I was ever going to share my fulcrum word in this book. Full disclosure, I do believe my fulcrum word is the "8" we should all agree upon. That said, a part of me doesn't want to share it right now, because I feel like that could be construed as being manipulative.

When I meet someone and ask what their fulcrum word is, I am very careful not to share mine. I want to be sure they make up their own Mind first. I have shared my word with some of my closest friends, and after discussing it a few times, some have agreed my word is the best. Isn't that what honest and wholesome persuasion is? Giving people all the information, and then let them make up their own Minds.

An example of me doing this is when my daughter went to church with me. During the sacrament she grabbed the juice, then the bread and was about to eat it, and I told her, "I wouldn't do that yet if I was you." She asked, "Why not?" I replied, "It's because you don't know or worship my God, or your mother's God, and that is for you to make up your own Mind, if or when you do." I love and accept her for being herself, not for performing the same actions as me.

It took me a long time to learn there is a right, a wrong, and a preference. Trying to force or coerce others to Believe your way is not giving their Minds and hearts their due. Did it even cross your Mind that they may be the ones in the right and you're the one in the wrong?

This is why we all need to take the Paradox Pill. Taking the Paradox Pill can help open our Mind(s) like a parachute, so we can hopefully see the optimal Paradigm, that empowers us to be the same yesterday, today, and tomorrow.

Bottom line, we want to be allowed to make our choices, it's only fair we allow others to make theirs. Then we both suffer or enjoy the consequences that come from those chosen actions. Checks & Balances.

Taking the Paradox pill can help open our Mind(s) like a parachute, so we can hopefully see the optimal Paradigm.

My hope is that by using Cube Philosophy, it will help you connect with this amazing life you are living. No one else can do it for you. You must choose to put in the effort, to engage, so you can make it into the best version of what you Believe you were made for. Working in harmony with your genetics, your individuality, and everyone else's.

I wish you all the best, dear reader. For those who have something to say, please comment on my website at www.cubephilosophy.com. I bet we will all benefit from hearing your input. That way we continue to grow and live this absurd and curious thing we call life, together.

To learn more about the Connection Cube and Cube Philosophy go to www.TheConnectionCube.com:

NOTES

NOTES

NOTES

NOTES

NOTES

NOTES

www.ingramcontent.com/pod-product-compliance
Lightning Source LLC
Chambersburg PA
CBHW061802070526
44586CB00023B/2674